P9-CQP-298

The Tent

Books by Margaret Atwood

FICTION

The Edible Woman

Surfacing

Lady Oracle

Dancing Girls

Life Before Man

Bodily Harm

Murder in the Dark

Bluebeard's Egg

The Handmaid's Tale

Cat's Eye

Wilderness Tips

Good Bones

The Robber Bride

Alias Grace

The Blind Assassin

Good Bones and Simple Murders

Oryx and Crake

The Penelopiad

The Tent

FOR CHILDREN

Up in the Tree

Anna's Pet (with Joyce Barkhouse)

For the Birds

Princess Prunella and the Purple Peanut

Rude Ramsay and the Roaring Radishes

Bashful Bob and Doleful Dorinda

NONFICTION

Survival: A Thematic Guide to Canadian Literature

Days of the Rebels 1815–1840

Second Words

Strange Things: The Malevolent North in Canadian Literature

Negotiating with the Dead: A Writer on Writing

Writing with Intent: Essays, Reviews, Personal Prose 1983–2005

POETRY

Double Persephone

The Circle Game

The Animals in That Country

The Journals of Susanna Moodie

Procedures for Underground

Power Politics

You Are Happy

Selected Poems

Two-Headed Poems

True Stories

Interlunar

Selected Poems II: Poems Selected and New 1976–1986

Morning in the Burned House

3 9504 00218979 9

The Tent

Margaret Atwood

Nan A. Talese

Doubleday

New York   London   Toronto   Sydney   Auckland

PUBLISHED BY NAN A. TALESE
AN IMPRINT OF DOUBLEDAY
a division of Random House, Inc.
1745 Broadway, New York, New York 10019

DOUBLEDAY is a registered trademark of Random House, Inc.

Book design by Caroline Cunningham

Library of Congress Cataloging-in-Publication Data

Atwood, Margaret Eleanor, 1939–
The tent / Margaret Atwood—1st ed.
p. cm.

I. Title.
PR9199.3.A8T46 2006
813'.54—dc22   2005043729

ISBN 0-385-51668-1

Copyright © 2006 by O.W. Toad, Ltd.

All Rights Reserved

PRINTED IN THE UNITED STATES OF AMERICA

February 2006

First Edition in the United States of America

1 3 5 7 9 10 8 6 4 2

For Graeme

Contents

I.

CONTENTS

II.

III.

CONTENTS

I.

Life Stories

Why the hunger for these? If it is a hunger. Maybe it's more like bossiness. Maybe we just want to be in charge, of the life, no matter who lived it.

It helps if there are photos. No more choices for the people in them – pick this one, dump that one. The livers of the lives in question had their chances, most of which they blew. They should have spotted the photographer in the bushes, they shouldn't have chewed with their mouths open, they shouldn't have worn the strapless top, they shouldn't have yawned, they shouldn't have laughed: so unattractive, the candid denture. *So that's what she looked like*, we say, connecting the snapshot to the year of the torrid affair. *Face like a half-eaten pizza, and is that him, gaping down her front? What did he see in her, besides cheap lunch? He was already going bald. What was all the fuss about?*

I'm working on my own life story. I don't mean I'm putting it together; no, I'm taking it apart. It's mostly a question of editing. If you'd wanted the narrative line you should have asked earlier, when I still knew everything and was more than willing to tell. That was before I discovered the virtues of scissors, the virtues of matches.

I was born, I would have begun, once. But snip, snip, away go mother and father, white ribbons of paper blown by the wind, with grandparents tossed out for good measure. *I spent my childhood*. Enough of that as well. Goodbye dirty little dresses, goodbye scuffed shoes that caused me such anguish, goodbye well-thumbed tears and scabby knees, and sadness worn at the edges.

Adolescence can be discarded too, with its salty tanned skin, its fecklessness and bad romance and leakages of seasonal blood. What was it like to breathe so heavily, as if drugged, while rubbing up against strange leather coats in alleyways? I can't remember.

Once you get started it's fun. So much free space opens up. Rip, crumple, up in flames, out the window.

I was born, I grew up, I studied, I loved, I married, I procreated, I said, I wrote, all gone now. *I went, I saw, I did.* Farewell crumbling turrets of historic interest, farewell icebergs and war monuments, all those young stone men with eyes upturned, and risky voyages teeming with germs, and dubious hotels, and doorways opening both in and out. Farewell friends and lovers, you've slipped from view, erased, defaced: I know you once had hairdos and told jokes, but I can't recall them. Into the ground with you, my tender fur-brained cats and dogs, and horses and mice as well: I adored you, dozens of you, but what were your names?

I'm getting somewhere now, I'm feeling lighter. I'm coming unstuck from scrapbooks, from albums, from diaries and journals, from space, from time. Only a paragraph left, only a sentence or two, only a whisper.

I was born.

I was.

I.

Clothing Dreams

Oh no. Not this again. It's the clothing dream. I've been having it for fifty years. Aisle after aisle, closetful after closetful, metal rack after metal rack of clothing, stretching into the distance under the glare of the fluo-rescent tubing – as gaudy and ornate and confusing, and finally as glum and oppressive, as the dreams of a long-time opium smoker. Why am I compelled to riffle through these outfits, tangling up the hangers, tripping on the ribbons, snagging myself on a hook or button while feathers and sequins and fake pearls drop to the floor like ants from a burning tree? What is the occa-sion? Who do I need to impress?

———

There's a smell of stale underarms. Everything's been worn before. Nothing fits. Too small, too big, too magenta. These flounces, hoops, ruffles, wired collars, cut-velvet capes – none of these disguises is mine. How old am I in this dream? Do I have tits? Whose life am I living? Whose life am I failing to live?

Bottle

— I only want to be like everyone else, I said.

— You're not, though, was what he told me. You're not like them.

— Why not? I said. I was inclined to listen to him. He had a persuasive manner.

— Because I love you.

— Is that all?

— I'm not just anyone, he said.

— Nobody is, I said.

— You see, he said, that's what I mean, you're not like everyone else. You notice the details, you take the distinguishing characteristics into account, you pick out the tendencies. These are the qualities I'm looking for.

— Is this a seduction? I said.

— No. The seduction took place a while ago; you didn't even notice it. We're past that. We're at the hiring stage. We've come to the bargaining.

— What do I have to do? I said.

— Sleep with me, that goes without saying. I'll make it worth your while.

— What else?

— I value loyalty. Remember, you're not a lawyer: don't fuck the clients.

— I wouldn't anyway. They always have bad karma. What else?

— Just what you're already doing, he said. Some routine chores. Inhale some smoke, chew selected plant materials, tell a couple of riddles, write things on leaves. Do the odd incantation; lead a few sightseeing tours of hell. Keep up the tone of the establishment.

— No fooling around with snakes? I can't, if there's snakes. I have a phobia.

— Snakes were last year.

— Good. Where do I sign? Just a minute – what do I get in return?

— Women are so mercenary.

— No, but seriously?

— You'll get wise. Wiser than you are, I mean.

— It's not enough.

— All right: you can have some immortality. Here it is. It's inside this bottle. See it?

— That little heap of dust?

— Look harder.

— Oh. Yes. Does it always sparkle like that?

— Only at first.

— Are you sure this is immortality?

— Trust me. With some of this, you'll always have a voice.

— Have a voice, or *be* a voice?

— One or the other.

— Well, okay, thanks a lot then.

— Don't drop the bottle. Be careful with it. You have to watch those things, they have a habit of getting bigger. They can get as big as the sky. You can be sucked into them before you know it. It's the vacuum effect. Now set it down, over there in the corner, dump that bulky mantle, and put your arms . . .

— I feel dizzy. This is getting a little intense. I ate too much at lunch. I think I should go home and lie down.

— Lie down right here! You owe me, remember? No time like the present. Slit a throat, pour a libation, empty your mind, close your eyes, clear a space for me, think about caves . . .

— Ouch. Let go! I need to breathe. I can't, right now. How about next week?

— Don't you love me?

— It's not that. It's just — are you really who you say you are?

— I am what I am. I'm also who you say I am. That's the way it is with gods, and I'm a god, after all.

— So there's nothing to you. You're only in my head. You're just a — you're nothing.

— More or less.

— That's what I thought. Wait, come back!

— I'm not stupid, I recognize *no* when I hear it.

— I didn't mean to be abrupt. Let's talk.

— You can't talk with nothing.

— But —

Impenetrable Forest

The person you have in mind is lost. That's the picture I'm getting. He believes he is lost in the middle of an impenetrable forest. His head is full of trees. Branches he's bumping into. Brambles he's tangled up in. Paths that lead nowhere. Animals that jeer at him and run away. Here and there the glimpse of an elusive maiden, wearing a dress of what appears to be white cheesecloth. I'm getting some insects too, the stinging variety. This is not pleasant. The sun is sinking. The shadows are darkening. Things could hardly be worse.

Then there's you. Where do you come into it? You're not one to resist an opportunity, the sort of opportunity he presents. Some would call it meddling, but you think

of it as helpfulness. I apologize for being so frank but I'm just the messenger. Here you come, descending in our pinkish cloud, glowing like a low-wattage light bulb or an aquarium in a chintzy bar. Feathers sprout from your shoulders, rays of light shoot out from you, silver-and-gold confetti wafts down from you like metallic dandruff. It does not occur to you that your dress is covered with tiny fish hooks. On some of them scraps of bait are still hanging: cricket wings, worm torsos, old bank deposit slips.

There there, you say. A whisk here, a flick there, with your magic wand – transparent plastic, with a miniature motorcar in it that slides up and down in a sparkly fluid when shaken – and the brambles vanish. The sun reverses direction, the paths straighten out, dawn occurs.

Voilà! you say. Your debts are paid, your emotional problems are solved, your illnesses are cured. Not only that, but your childhood sorrows – the ones that held you back and bogged you down – they've been erased. Now you can get on with it.

He looks at you without gratitude. What is this *it* I'm supposed to be getting on with? he says.

You don't know? you ask, with an irritation you try to conceal. I've come down into this stupid woodlot, gone to major trouble, cleared away a lifetime of junk for you, and you still don't know?

You don't understand much, he says. Why do you think I was lost in the impenetrable forest in the first place?

Encouraging the Young

I have decided to encourage the young. Once I wouldn't have done this, but now I have nothing to lose. The young are not my rivals. Fish are not the rivals of stones.

So I will encourage them open-handedly, I will encourage them en masse. I'll fling encouragement over them like rice at a wedding. They are *the young*, a collective noun, like *the electorate*. I'll encourage them indiscriminately, whether they deserve it or not. Anyway, I can't tell them apart.

So I will stand cheering generally, like a blind person at a football game: noise is what is required, waves of it, invigorating yelps to inspire them to greater efforts, and who cares on what side and to what ends?

I don't mean the very young, those who can still display their midriffs without attracting derision. Boredom's their armour: to them I'm a voice balloon with nothing in it.

No. It's the newly conscious young I mean, the ones with ambition and fresh diffidence, those who've learned the hard way that reach exceeds grasp nine times out of ten. How disappointed they are! And if and when they succeed for the first time, how anxious it makes them! They develop insomnia, or claustrophobia, or bulimia, or fear of heights. Now they will have to live up to themselves. Bummer.

Here I am, happy to help! I'll pass round the encouragement, a cookie's worth for each. There you are, young! What is a big, stupid, clumsy mess like the one you just made — let me rephrase that — what is an understandable human error, but a learning experience? Try again! Follow your dream! You can do it!

What a fine and shining person I am, so much kinder than when I'd just finished being young myself. I was severe then; my standards were exacting. The young — I felt — were allowed to get away with far too much, as I had been. But now I'm generosity itself. Affably I smile and dole.

On second thought, my motives are less pure than

they appear. They are murkier. They are lurkier. I catch sight of myself, in that inward eye that is not always the bliss of solitude, and I see that I am dubious. I scuttle from bush to bush, at the edge of the dark woods, peering out. *Yoo hoo! Young! Over here!* I call, beckoning with my increasingly knobbly forefinger. *That's it! Now, here's a lavish gingerbread house, decorated with your name in lights. Wouldn't you like to walk into it, claim it as your own, stuff your face on sugary fame? Of course you would!*

I won't fatten them in cages, though. I won't ply them with poisoned fruit items. I won't change them into clockwork images or talking shadows. I won't drain out their life's blood. They can do all those things for themselves.

Voice

I was given a voice. That's what people said about me. I cultivated my voice, because it would be a shame to waste such a gift. I pictured this voice as a hothouse plant, something luxuriant, with glossy foliage and the word *tuberous* in the name, and a musky scent at night. I made sure the voice was provided with the right temperature, the right degree of humidity, the right ambience. I soothed its fears; I told it not to tremble. I nurtured it, I trained it, I watched it climb up inside my neck like a vine.

The voice bloomed. People said I had grown into my voice. Soon I was sought after, or rather my voice was. We went everywhere together. What people saw was me, what I saw was my voice, ballooning out in front of me like the translucent greenish membrane of a frog in full trill.

My voice was courted. Bouquets were thrown to it. Money was bestowed on it. Men fell on their knees before it. Applause flew around it like flocks of red birds.

Invitations to perform cascaded over us. All the best places wanted us, and all at once, for, as people said – though not to me – my voice would thrive only for a certain term. Then, as voices do, it would begin to shrivel. Finally it would drop off, and I would be left alone, denuded – a dead shrub, a footnote.

It's begun to happen, the shrivelling, Only I have noticed it so far. There's the barest pucker in my voice, the barest wrinkle. Fear has entered me, a needleful of ether, constricting what in someone else would be my heart.

Now it's evening; the neon lights come on, excitement quickens in the streets. We sit in this hotel room, my voice and I; or rather in this hotel suite, because it's still nothing but the best for us. We're gathering our strength together. How much of my life do I have left? Left over, that is: my voice has used up most of it. I've given it all my love, but it's only a voice, it can never love me in return.

Although it's begun to decay, my voice is still as greedy as ever. Greedier: it wants more, more and more, more of everything it's had so far. It won't let go of me easily.

Soon it will be time for us to go out. We'll attend a luminous occasion, the two of us, chained together as always. I'll put on its favourite dress, its favourite neck-lace. I'll wind a fur around it, to protect it from the drafts. Then we'll descend to the foyer, glittering like ice, my voice attached like an invisible vampire to my throat.

No More Photos

No more photos. Surely there are enough. No more shadows of myself thrown by light onto pieces of paper, onto squares of plastic. No more of my eyes, mouths, noses, moods, bad angles. No more yawns, teeth, wrinkles. I suffer from my own multiplicity. Two or three images would have been enough, or four, or five. That would have allowed for a firm idea: *This is she.* As it is, I'm watery, I ripple, from moment to moment I dissolve into my other selves. Turn the page: you, looking, are newly confused. You know me too well to know me. Or not too well: too much.

Orphan Stories

i) How swiftly the orphans set sail! No sooner does the
starting gun fire than they're flying! Their yachts are
slimmer, their lines trimmer than ours — than our
stodgy barges. They drag no anchors, they haul no
ballast, they toss all baggage overboard, and the one flag
they ever hoist is blank. No wonder they pull out of the
bay ahead of the rest, no wonder they round the cape so
briskly! But what now? They won't stay on course, they
won't play by the well-wrought rules, they despise the
prize. They're headed for the open sea. They're sailing
into the sun. They're gone.

———

ii) Orphans have bad experiences: in barns, in cellars, in automobiles, in woodsheds, in vacant fields, in empty classrooms. It's because they're so tempting. It's because they're so damaged. It's because they're so scrawny. It's because they're so easily broken. It's because they're so available. It's because they're so erotic. It's because no one will believe what they say.

iii) The orphans line up for their gruel. All kinds of orphans – car-crash orphans, boat-accident orphans, heart-attack orphans, unwed-mother orphans, war orphans – for all of these gruel is provided, out of the goodness of our hearts. They don't get much, a dollop here, a dollop there, but such is the way, in orphanages. They wait for their dollops, standing quietly in their cheap grey uniforms, provided by us as well. How kind we are, how virtuous we feel! One day the orphans start banging with their cheap tin spoons, on their cheap tin plates. They've been told to be thankful, to be grateful, not to be greedy, but they want more. They want more and more and more. They want what we have! How dare they? How dare they brandish their hunger at us like a sword?

———

iv) What are their names? Names are arbitrary, but orphans' names are more arbitrary than most. They make up their names as they go along. Call me Ishmael, they say. Or else: Call me Ishmael, but call me often. Or else: Don't call me Ishmael, call me Anonymous. Call me No-name. Call me In Vain. Orphans are such flirts, they'll hook up with anyone, then they tear up their phone books, they discard at random. They show no mercy.

v) *You're not my real parents*, every child has thought. *I'm not your real child.* But with orphans, it's true. What freedom, to thumb your nose authentically! For orphans, all roads are open. For orphans, all roads are the one not chosen. For orphans, all roads are necessary. How can they be kicked out of home? They're out of home already. They hitch through life, one casual ride after another. Their rule is the rule of thumb.

vi) On the other hand how sad, to make your way like a snail, a very fast snail but a snail nonetheless, with no home but the one on your back, and that home an empty shell. A home filled with nothing but yourself. It's heavy, that lightness. It's crushing, that emptiness.

vii) But what love they inspire, these orphans! Little orphan babies left in shopping bags, on doorsteps, in the cold. Little orphan babies left in baskets, under cabbage leaves, by birds, by cupids, by gnomes. Folks line up for them, cross-eyed with pity, money in their pockets, damp handkerchiefs in their fists, rescue in their minds, blankets in their knapsacks, warm arms open, waiting to gather them in. *Where did you come from, baby dear?* Out of the darkness. Out of the fear.

viii) Nevertheless, we're warned against them, these orphans. They're sly, they're shifty. How do you know anything about them? Who were their people? Bar the doors, hide the silver! If you find a baby in the bulrushes, leave it there! Don't invite the orphans over your threshold! They'll cut your throat for a penny, they'll run off with your daughter, they'll seduce your son, they'll wreck your home, because home is where the heart is and the orphans are heartless.

———

ix) No, you've got it wrong. It's the other way around. The orphans are not the stealers but the stolen; they are not the killers but the killed. You can tell where the orphans have wandered by the trails they leave: bread-crumbs in the forest, drops of blood, tears that have turned into small white mushrooms, small piles of fragile bones among the roots and moss.

Read the statistics: their chances are not good. Their stepmothers demand their tongues on a plate; their fathers have skipped town; their uncles send villains with pillows to smother them in their sleep. It's only in books – and only some books – that a generous benefactor appears in the nick of time to save the orphans from the forces of malice ranged against them. What are those forces? Look into the magic mirror, sweet reader. Look into the deep still wishing well. Ask yourself.

x) It's a good excuse, though, orphanhood. It explains everything – every mistake and wrong turn. As Sherlock Holmes declared, *She had no mother to advise her.* How we long for it, that lack of advice! Imprudence could have been ours. Passionate affairs. Reckless adventures. Of course we're grateful for our stable upbringings, our hordes of informative relatives, our fleece-lined advantages, our lack of dramatic plots. But there's a corner of envy in us all the same. Why doesn't anything of interest happen to us, coddled as we are? Why do the orphans get all the good lines?

xi) Now the letters will arrive, from orphans. *How could you treat orphanhood so lightly!* they will say. *You don't understand what it's like to be an orphan. You are the sort of person who jeers at those with no legs. You are frivolous and cruel. You are harsh.*

Ah yes, dear orphans, I can see how you would feel that way. But to note is not to disparage. All observations of life are harsh, because life is. I lament that fact, but I cannot change it.

(And consider: It is loss to which everything flows, absence in which everything flowers. It is you, not we, who have always been the children of the gods.)

Gateway

You were led to expect a road, a river, a boat, a gate, a guardian. All were supplied, though none was what you'd imagined. The road was indistinguishable from many of the sidewalks you'd so often trudged along: poured concrete, dirty in the usual way – weathered chewing gum, fresh spit, the odd dog dropping. Your feet were tired – whose shoes were you wearing? – but there was no place to sit down. The river, when you came to it, was a canal, stagnant with algae and floating plastic bags. A shabby houseboat was moored there, but no path led down to it. Instead the sidewalk took you across a massive iron bridge, painted grey. After that came a red brick wall that went on for a long time. It had posters stuck onto it – a play was being advertised, or else a film – the same poster, over and over. They showed a woman's face with a surprised expression, her hand raised as if in self-protection, with big lettering in blue and orange and lines of smaller print: favourable quotations from the newspapers, no doubt, but somehow you couldn't read them. In addition to the posters there were names spray-painted on the brick – no one you knew – and hot-pink symbol-writing that suggested the twisted-balloon animals made by clowns at children's parties.

At last came the gate. It had a door, a steel door set into the brick wall. It was dented, as if people had been kicking at it with heavy boots. The guardian was leaning against it. He had the look of a man who'd been sleeping rough for some time. Old jeans, stubbled face, broken sandals; a torn rucksack by his feet.

You got here at last, he said. These are your things. I've kept them for you.

My things? you said. You inspected the rucksack. It didn't look familiar. What did he mean by things? A toothbrush, underwear?

Things you saved up, he said. For this occasion.

You lifted the rucksack. It was very light. You wondered if there was a sandwich in it. You weren't hungry, but you might be later. You examined the door. There were no windows in it. There was no lock.

I'm supposed to go in here? you said.

I have to ask you some questions first, he said. Think carefully before you answer.

All right, you said. You had an idea about the questions: you'd be asked to give a good account of yourself, and to admit to your misdeeds, such as they were. You thought you were ready. You hadn't been perfect, but then, perfection wouldn't be expected. Surely not, or who would ever get in?

Here are the questions, he said. What is your favourite colour? Did you love your cat? Did you ever find a coin on the pavement? Were you happy?

Suddenly it's the present tense. The first question baffles you. Do you have a favourite colour or not? You can't remember. Everything you've been meaning to say in your own defence has gone right out of your head. Now a wind has begun to blow: ripped posters whirl along the street, open mouths, hands, eyes. Perhaps you should open the rucksack. You never had a cat. What do coins have to do with it? There must be some mistake.

Bottle II

Bring your ear down closer. Put your hand over the other ear. Think of seashells. There. Now you can hear me.

It must be a surprise for you, the discovery that there's a voice inside this bottle. You thought you were buying a curio, which is what most people would call a round-bodied glass object, ornate, dusty, out of date, filled with layers of coloured sand, purple-pink-orange-green-beige. A sort of ornament. A sort of souvenir, from a place you haven't in fact ever visited.

———

Then you saw the sand moving, in a bottle with the cork in. At first you thought it might be an earthquake, a small one, the kind that rattles teacups. But no. You watched closely. You were not mistaken: yes, there was a rippling, a shivering, a wavelet of purple sand. Some sort of insect life, perhaps. You took out the cork.

That was when you heard the voice. My voice, to be precise. It was a small sibilant voice, like the rustling of old corn husks in a breeze, or of dried leaves kept for eons in a cave. It was a hissing, like steam escaping fitfully from a fissure in damp mud. An underground sound, hinting of unknown pressures, of unknown powers. It was an enticing whisper.

Ask me what you need to know, this voice — my voice — promised. Ask and I'll tell you. Your car keys? They're under the bed. Your stock holdings? I see gold, but is it yours? Your death, when and where? This voice offered you knowledge, but also fear. Fear is synonymous with the future, and the future consists of forked roads, I should say forking roads, because the roads are forking all the time, like slow lightning. A road is a process, not a location. I can put my fingertips on this road, on these roads, on this trembling branchwork, my fingertips that are now so fine and spidery.

How did it come to this? My present arachnid state. I was young once, I was beautiful, I was sought after, I had picturesque robes and exceptional talents. I uttered portents in caves: there were lineups, there were waiting lists for them. How did I come to be so tiny, so translucent, so wispy, so whispery? How did I come to be shut up inside this bottle? It's an unusual story, an incredible story, a story that could not take place today. I'm not sure I still believe it myself, though I'll tell it to anyone who'll lend an ear.

Right now that means you. I am not a curio, my friend. Or rather I am a curio, but you'd have to say *the* curio, the best one of all. Only the very curious acquire curios like this. And you are a curious person, you look into the medicine cabinets in the bathrooms of people you hardly know, you're an avid listener, you're driven to listen, you'll listen to anything. I understand you: I too was curious once, like you. We are both the kind of person who takes the corks out of bottles. Not bottles of wine: bottles of sand.

II.

Winter's Tales

Once upon a time, you say, there were germs with horns. They lived in the toilet and could only be defeated by gallons and gallons of bleach. You could commit suicide by drinking this bleach, and some women did.

The young look up at you, wide-eyed. Or maybe they look down at you: they've become very tall. How young are the young, these days? It varies. Some of them are quite old. But they are still credulous, because you were there, once upon a time, and they weren't.

Not only that, you say – you're enjoying this – there were no bare midriffs, and only sailors and convicts had tattoos. There were no telephones, there were no vaccinations; so you couldn't call the doctor when you were dying, of burst glands, of stagnant intestinal bloats, of webs inside your throat, of brain fever. If you had unprotected intercourse your nose dropped off, a lot sooner than it does now.

The young are still listening. Do they believe you? Have you been sensational enough for them? You certainly hope so.

If you were a married woman, it was all over at thirty, you say. You were doomed to put on a print dress and a rubber girdle and sit in a rocking chair on the porch – there were porches, back then – fanning yourself, because there was no air conditioning, and talking about your flat feet, your sciatica, your varicose veins, and the snoring habits of your husband, whose shirts you had to iron, every Tuesday – mountains of shirts. All of these were metaphors for unsatisfactory sex.

At this there are a few giggles. But you don't want the past to be taken lightly: it cost too much. It deserves respect. So now it's time for the serious artillery.

Let me tell you about meat loaf, you say, lowering your voice, as the already pale faces around you turn ashen. Yes – meat loaf! Meat loaf, and enemas, and bulb-headed syringes used for what they called "feminine hygiene" – the three are not unconnected, you say, in a thrilling whisper.

By now the young are staring at you with fascinated horror, as if you're about to pull off one of your legs, revealing a green and mossy amputated stump. War stories, that's what they want — war stories, and disgusting menus. They want suffering, they want scars. Shall you tell them about pot roast?

But that might be going too far. Anyway, you've excited yourself enough for one evening.

It's Not Easy Being Half-Divine

Helen lived down the street from me when we were growing up. We used to sell Kool-Aid off her front porch, five cents a glass, and she always had to be the one to carry the glass down the steps, eyelids lowered and with that pink bow in her hair, and mincing along like she was walking on eggs. I think she palmed a few nickels, being hardly the most honest type. I know she's famous and all now, but quite frankly she was a pain in the butt then and still is. She used to tell the worst lies — said her dad was somebody really high up, not the Pope but close, and of course we teased her about that. Not that this so-called big shot ever showed his face. Her mum was just another single mother, as they call them now, but my own mum says they had another name for it once. She said they had goings-on at night around there, naturally, since every man in town thought it was being handed out for free. Used to throw pebbles at the door, shout names and howl a bit when they got drunk. The two boys, Helen's brothers – they were pretty wild, they took off early.

When she was ten, Helen went through a circus phase – liked to dress up, thought she'd be a trapeze artist – then she got close with the woman who ran the beauty salon, used to do her hair for her and give her product samples, and then she started drawing black rims around her eyes and hanging around the bus station. Fishing for a ticket out of town, is my guess. She was good-looking – I'll grant her that – so it wasn't surprising she got married early, to the police chief, a prime catch for both of them as he was pushing forty.

Then just a few months ago she ran off with some man from the city who was passing through. Didn't need the bus ticket after all, he had his own car, quite the boat. Hubby's pissed as hell; he's talking about a posse, go into the city, smoke them out, beat the guy up, get her back, smack her around a bit. A lot of men wouldn't bother, with a tramp like that; but it seems he doesn't believe in divorce, says somebody has to stand for the right values.

Personally I think he's still nuts about her and anyway his pride is hurt. Trouble is she's flaunting it — the new man's quite well off, set her up in some sort of mansion, her picture gets in magazines and people asking about her opinions, it's enough to make you sick. So there she is, all diddied up in her new pearl necklace and smiling away as sweet as pie and saying how happy she is in her new life, and how every woman should follow her heart. Says it wasn't easy when she was growing up, being half-divine and all, but now she's come to terms with it and she's looking at a career in the movies. Says she was too young to get married that first time but now she knows how fulfilling love can be, and the chief wasn't, well, he just wasn't. Of course everyone thinks she's saying he was a nothing in the sack department, so there's been some snickering up the sleeves, though not openly because he's still got a lot of clout in this town.

The long and the short of it is, pardon my pun, nobody likes to be laughed at. The chief's from a big family, a brother and a lot of cousins, all of them with muscles and tempers. My bet is things will get serious. It's worth watching.

Salome Was a Dancer

Salome went after the Religious Studies teacher. It was really mean of her, he wasn't up to her at all, no more sense of self-protection than a zucchini, always droning on about morality and so forth, but he'd finger the grapefruits in the supermarket in this creepy way, a grapefruit in each hand, he'd stand there practically drooling, one of those gaunt-looking men who'd fall on his knees if a woman ever looked at him seriously, but so far none of them had. As I say it was really mean of her, but he'd failed her on her mid-term and she was under pressure at home, they wanted her to perform as they put it, so I guess she thought this would be a shortcut.

Anyway, with a mother like hers what could you

expect? Divorced, remarried, bracelets all up her arms and fake eyelashes out to here, and pushy as hell. Started entering Salome in those frilly-panty beauty contests when she was five, tap-dance lessons, the lot, they'd slather the makeup on those poor tots and teach them to wiggle their little behinds, what a display. And then her stepdad ran the biggest bank in town so I guess she thought she could get away with anything. I wouldn't be surprised if there wasn't some hanky-panky going on in that direction too, the way she'd bat her baby blues at him and wheedle, sickening to watch her rubbing up against him and cooing, he'd promised her a Porsche when she turned sixteen.

She was Tinker Bell in the school play when she was twelve, I certainly remember that. Seven layers of cheesecloth was all she wore, there was supposed to be a body stocking underneath but whether there was or not, your guess is as good as mine. And all those middle-aged dads sitting with their legs crossed. Oh, she knew what she was doing!

Anyway, when she got the rotten mark in Religious Studies she went to work on the guy, who knows how it started but when they were caught together in the stock-room she had her shirt off. The teacher was growling away at her bra, having trouble with the hooks, or so the story goes, you have to laugh. If you want what's in the package you should at least know how to get the string off, is what I say. Anyway, big scandal, and then he started badmouthing her, said she was a little slut and she'd led him on, did some innuendo on the mother just for good measure. Everyone believed him of course, but you always knew with Salome that if anyone's head was going to roll it wouldn't be hers. She accused the poor jerk of sexual assault, and since she was technically a minor – and of course her banker stepdad threw his weight around – she made it stick. Last seen, the guy was panhandling in the subway stations, down there in Toronto; grown a beard, looks like Jesus, crazy as a bedbug. Lost his head completely.

Salome didn't come to a good end either. Tried out for ballet school, Modern Dance was what she thought would suit her, show a lot of skin, centre your thoughts on the pelvis, bare feet, fling yourself about, but she didn't get in. Left home after some sort of blowup between the mom and the stepdad, midnight yelling about Miss Princess and her goings-on, furniture was thrown. After that she took to stripping in bars, just to annoy them I bet. Got whacked in her dressing room one night, right before the show, too bad for Management, someone clobbered her over the head with a vase, nothing on but her black leather macramé bikini and that steel-studded choke collar, used to get the clients all worked up, not that I'd know personally. Saw two guys running out the stage door in bicycle-courier outfits, some sort of uniform anyway, never caught them though. Hit men set on by the stepdad is one rumour, wild with jealousy. Guys get like that when their hair falls out. It was all the mother's fault, if you ask me.

Plots for Exotics

From an early age I knew my ambition was to be in a plot. Or several plots — I thought of it as a career. But no plots came my way. You have to apply for them, a friend of mine told me. He'd been around, though he hadn't been in any plots himself, so I took his advice and went down to the plot factory. As for everything else, there was an interview. So, said the youngish bored man behind the desk, you think you've got what it takes to be in a plot. What sort of character did you have in mind? He was fiddling with a list, running his felt-tip pen down it. Character? I said. Yes, that's what we do here. Plots and characters. You can't have one without the other. Well, I said, I might as well try out for the main character. Or one of them – I suppose every plot needs more than one. You can't be a main character, he said bluntly. Why not? I said. Look in the mirror, he said. You're an exotic. What do you mean, an exotic? I said. I'm a respectable person. I don't do kinky dancing. *Exotic*, he said in his bored voice. Consult the dictionary. Alien, foreign, coming in from the outside. Not from here. But I am from here, I said. Do I have a funny accent or something? I don't make the rules, he said. Maybe you are, I'm not denying it, but your appearance is against it. If we were in some other place you wouldn't look as if you'd come in from the outside, because you'd already be outside, and so would everyone else there. Then I'd be the exotic, wouldn't I? He gave a short laugh. But we're here, aren't we. Here we are. And there *you* are. I wasn't ready to argue about who looked like where, so I said, Okay then, not the main character. What else have you got? For exotics, he said, flipping through the pages of his list. Let me see. There didn't used to be much of a choice. You could be a jovial, well-meaning exotic, or a stupid, drunken, wife-beating abuser of an exotic, or a hostile exotic falling off a horse, or a clever, malevolent exotic with some kind of big evil plan. If you were a woman, you could be a sexy exotic – a smouldering, beautiful, amoral degenerate. On the other hand, you could be a comical servant. That was it. That was it? I said. I was dismayed. But there's more options now, he said. His manner was warming up. You could be the best friend, he said. You wouldn't get the girl, but at least you'd get a girl of some sort. Or you could be the next-door neighbour, drop by for friendly chats. Or you could be some guy with lore — sort of like a coach. Teach the main character how to slice off heads, one-handed, with a sword. We can always use those. Or you could be a wise person; you could have, like, an ancient religion, or you could say meaningful but obscure things, issue what-do-you-call thems. Portents, I said. Yes, he said, like that. Once you only had to be a woman to get those wise parts, any kind of a woman, but then women started having jobs and no one could believe they were wise any more. Nowadays if you're a wise woman you have to be an exotic woman. You can have wisdom if you're a man, but you have to be old as well. Beards help. Can you sing? Not particularly, I said. Too bad, he said. The opera's out, then. Lots of plots there. I could've put you in the chorus. They don't care what anyone looks like. They all wear those exotic outfits anyway. Listen, I said. None of this sounds like me. It doesn't exactly call out. How about getting me a job in the plot factory? I think I'd be good at that. What? he said. He sounded alarmed.

I'd get the hang of it really fast, I said. I could make up some new plots, or give a twist or two to the old ones — move the characters around a few slots. Give some other people a crack at playing the drunken idiots and the comic servants and so on. Increase their dramatic range. What I was really thinking was, I'd be able to rope off a main character or two for myself. Fulfill my child-hood dreams. Or I could do a whole plot with nothing in it but exotics. Exotics wall to wall. Then I'd be the main character for sure, no question.

He narrowed his eyes. Maybe he was reading my mind: I'm not very devious, I've always been bad at concealing things. I don't know, he said. We have standards to keep up. I don't think it would work.

Resources of the Ikarians

A country needs a resource, and ours does not have one. No oil wells, no mineral deposits, no diamonds, no forests, no rich topsoil, no fast-running rivers available for electrical power. How could we have such resources, stuck far out in the ocean on a barren goat-infested lump of geology at a point equidistant from all places of importance?

We have, it is true, some history. In the old days, before radar, a lot of ships were wrecked on our shifting reefs and unreliable shoals. Our ancestors did quite well out of that, moving the beacons around, raiding the shattered holds, robbing the corpses. We've tried to make this history into a resource, without much result.

The distances tourists must travel in order to view the narrow, stone-covered beaches where these deplorable outrages occurred are too great, the prices therefore too high. We've erected a few ruins, but they are not convincing, even from a distance.

Some accounts of us – in the more outmoded and spurious travel books – cite a legend according to which our island came into being – through the act of some god or other – at the point where the Icarus famed in Greek myth plunged into the sea, once his artificial wax wings had melted. This mistake arose from the name of our island: a word not, in fact, even faintly Greek. It means – in our language – simply "wad of mud." But the resorts – or the former resorts, built by hopeful foreign investors – resorts that invariably closed down halfway into their second season, after which we locals nicked the toilets – these resorts tried to capitalize on the romantic falsehood, and stuck a boy with wings on their notepaper. A scorched boy in the act of plummeting to his death, I should add. As a logo it was not well thought out.

What are we to do? The child sex trade is not for us: our children are unattractive and rude, and – due to their knowledge of our history – have a bad habit of mugging prospective customers and shoving them over cliffs. We've tried to work up some local handicrafts: we taught the old women to do tatting – they had a vestigial memory of it – but who wants tatting nowadays? Not even our line of tatted bikinis was successful. We took a crack at Internet telemarketing, which allowed us to raid carelessly guarded credit-card accounts; we've always been hard to get at, legally, being so far away from anything resembling a court of law. We also had a period of virtual airline reservation booking, shut down after too many rage-fuelled manslaughters in the business-class lounge; and we tried a fast-food chain specializing in goatburgers, for which we failed to create a vogue. Also we ran out of goats. So what now, we ask ourselves? Our labour force is not numerous, and is in any case averse to labouring. What we would really like is some offshore banks, or else a penal institution, but those do not grow on trees.

In our desperation we've fallen back on the idea of artists. Surely we have enough misery in store to produce a crop of these. Out of the pain we've taken care to inflict on them during their childhoods and at random intervals thereafter, out of the poverty we can guarantee, the artists will make art. They will write or paint or sing and then they will die early, and after that we can cash in. Postcards will be ours, black-and-white ones in which the artist frowns or scowls; pilgrimages too, and places of interest (the artist's birthplace, with a blue enamel plaque on it; his local bar, ditto; his favourite sleeping ditch); tasteless figurines of the artist made out of wire coat-hangers; perhaps – is it too much to ask? – a coffee-table book. In the far distance, a film, in which the artist suffers and scowls and drinks and dies young all over again. But this plan hasn't worked out yet.

We did have a poet who almost won a prize. He kicked the bucket last year, helped along by drink and drugs, and also by some of us. We may have been in too much of a hurry – perhaps we should have let him ripen a bit longer – but a living impoverished poet is a drain on the economy, whereas a dead one has potential.

We have hopes, however. Our greatest resource is surely our optimism: a tribute to the human spirit, you might call it. Already the T-shirt makers have swung into action. All is not lost.

Our Cat Enters Heaven

Our cat was raptured up to heaven. He'd never liked heights, so he tried to sink his claws into whatever invisible snake, giant hand, or eagle was causing him to rise in this manner, but he had no luck.

When he got to heaven, it was a large field. There were a lot of little pink things running around that he thought at first were mice. Then he saw God sitting in a tree. Angels were flying here and there with their fluttering white wings; they were making sounds like doves. Every once in a while God would reach out with its large furry paw and snatch one of them out of the air and crunch it up. The ground under the tree was littered with bitten-off angel wings.

Our cat went politely over to the tree.

Meow, said our cat.

Meow, said God. Actually it was more like a roar.

I always thought you were a cat, said our cat, but I wasn't sure.

In heaven all things are revealed, said God. This is the form in which I choose to appear to you.

I'm glad you aren't a dog, said our cat. Do you think I could have my testicles back?

Of course, said God. They're over behind that bush.

Our cat had always known his testicles must be somewhere. One day he'd woken up from a fairly bad dream and found them gone. He'd looked everywhere for them – under sofas, under beds, inside closets – and all the time they were here, in heaven! He went over to the bush, and, sure enough, there they were. They reattached themselves immediately.

Our cat was very pleased. Thank you, he said to God.

God was washing its elegant long whiskers. De rien, said God.

Would it be possible for me to help you catch some of those angels? said our cat.

You never liked heights, said God, stretching itself out along the branch, in the sunlight. I forgot to say there was sunlight.

True, said our cat. I never did. There were a few disconcerting episodes he preferred to forget. Well, how about some of those mice?

They aren't mice, said God. But catch as many as you like. Don't kill them right away. Make them suffer.

You mean, play with them? said our cat. I used to get in trouble for that.

It's a question of semantics, said God. You won't get in trouble for that here.

Our cat chose to ignore this remark, as he did not know what "semantics" was. He did not intend to make a fool of himself. If they aren't mice, what are they? he said. Already he'd pounced on one. He held it down under his paw. It was kicking, and uttering tiny shrieks.

They're the souls of human beings who have been bad on Earth, said God, half-closing its yellowy-green eyes. Now if you don't mind, it's time for my nap.

What are they doing in heaven then? said our cat.

Our heaven is their hell, said God. I like a balanced universe.

Chicken Little Goes Too Far

Chicken Little read too many newspapers. He listened to the radio too much, and he watched too much television. One day something snapped. What was the final straw? Hard to say, but whatever it was it shouldn't have made him hysterical. Most folks take such things in stride because whining is so unattractive, but not Chicken Little. He always had a short fuse. He went running down the street, cheeping at the top of his lungs. The sky is falling! he cheeped.

Oh for heavens' sakes, said Henny Penny, who was loading groceries into her four-wheel-drive supervan. Chicken Little, this is a public place. You're making a nuisance of yourself.

But the sky is falling! said Chicken Little. I'm sounding the alarm.

You sounded the exact same alarm last year, said Henny Penny, and the sky is still in place. Last time I looked, she added, with heavy irony.

"The sky is falling" is a metaphor, said Chicken Little huffily. It's true that the sky really is falling, but the falling of the sky represents all sorts of other things that are falling as well. Falling down, and falling apart. You should wake up!

Go home, have a beer, do some meditation, said Henny Penny. Whatever. You'll feel better tomorrow.

But the next day came and Chicken Little did not feel better. He dropped in on his old friend Turkey Lurkey, who taught at an institution of higher learning.

The sky is falling, said Chicken Little.

That's one analysis, said Turkey Lurkey. But there's data to show it isn't the sky that's falling. It's the earth that's rising. The rising of the earth is simply displacing the sky. It's due to natural geocyclical causes and is not the result of human activity, and therefore there is nothing we can do about it.

I don't see that it makes a blind bit of difference whether the earth is rising or the sky is falling, said

Chicken Little, as the end result in either case will be that we are minus a sky.

That is a simple-minded view, said Turkey Lurkey, with offensive condescension.

Chicken Little slammed Turkey Lurkey's office door, causing Turkey Lurkey's corkboard decorated with clever newspaper cartoons to fall onto the floor. Then he took himself off to Goosey Loosey, his old roommate, who was now the editor of a major newspaper.

The sky is falling, said Chicken Little. It's your duty to write an editorial about it!

If you'd said, "The stock market is falling," that would be news, said Goosey Loosey. Granted the sky is falling, in parts. We're not unaware of it, but the experts are working on it. They'll have a fix very soon. Meanwhile, no need to trigger a panic.

Chicken Little went away, disconsolate. He took refuge in a bar. He had a few drinks.

Drowning your sorrows? said the bartender, whose name was Skunky Punky.

The sky is falling, said Chicken Little.

They all say that, said Skunky Punky. The bitch not treating you right? So get a different chick, if you want my opinion. Play some golf. Work off some energy. Do you good.

Golf greens have toxic chemicals on them that will give you cancer of the gonads, said Chicken Little.

What sort of bullshit tree-hugging crapola you giving me? said Skunky Punky, who was tired of his job and wanted to pick a fight.

Excuse me, said Ducky Lucky, who'd been eavesdropping. I couldn't help overhearing. I'm the president of a lobby group dedicated to solving the very same sky-oriented deficiencies that appear to be disturbing you. It's not something you can take on alone. Together we can make a difference! Got your chequebook handy?

Chicken Little rejected this kind offer of assistance. He formed a group of his own, called TSIF – an acronym for The Sky Is Falling, as he had to explain carefully to journalists, at first. He launched a Web site. Soon he had a dedicated pack of disciples. They were mostly woodchucks and muskrats, but who cared? They picketed political gatherings. They blocked highways. They disrupted summit conferences. They carried big signs: Take Back the Sky! No Sky, No Pie, No Sweet Bye and Bye! The Sky's Our Limit!

This is getting serious, said Hoggy Groggy, who was head of a large development company that sold retirement-home properties in the sky. He himself lived in a bunker designed to protect him from the large chunks of sky that were now falling at random intervals and in unpredictable locations.

He called in Foxy Loxy. Foxy Loxy moved in the shadow world. He did nasty things for a price, and was a devotee of zero accountability. Guy's gotta put food on the table, was his motto. Not that he bothered much with tables. As far as he was concerned they were a frill.

This Chicken What's-his-name twerp is making a dent, Hoggy Groggy told Foxy Loxy. He's giving me a headache. He's against progress. You should put him out of his misery.

I eat guys like that for breakfast, said Foxy Loxy. It's the best method. There's no mess except maybe a couple of feathers, and they never find the body. What'll you pay me?

The sky's the limit, said Hoggy Groggy.

And so it was.

Thylacine Ragout

They cloned the Thylacine. They got some DNA out of a bone and they emptied the nucleus out of the egg of a Tasmanian devil and they put the Thylacine bone DNA into the egg, and it grew, and they implanted it, and it didn't work, and they did it again, and it didn't work, and they did it again, again, again, and they tried it a little differently, and they tweaked it this way and that, and finally they cloned the Thylacine. Out it came, the baby Thylacine, and they nurtured it tenderly and with great interest and there it was, running around with stripes on, frantic, as in the only remaining film of it, where it runs and paces and utters silent yelps because the film is a silent film, and it stops to gaze into the camera with an expression both poignant and severe. It was a Thylacine all right, or it looked like one, or it looked like our idea of one, because it was an animal no one still alive had ever actually seen. Anyway, what they got was close enough. Why quibble?

This event made the headlines, of course it did, and they named the Thylacine Trugannini, a name you see on restaurant menus in that part of the world, as a gesture of respect perhaps, or a way of selling something, or a commemoration, as on tombstones. Anyway, they named it Trugannini, after the last fully Aboriginal inhabitant of that island, who was raped, or that is the story, whose sisters were killed, or that is the story, whose mother was killed, whose husband was killed in front of her eyes, whose father died of grief, who lived in solitude, solitude of a kind that would kill most people, whose bones were dug up and put on display for a hundred years, against her will, but she was dead so what will did she have, what right do the dead have to a will, they are dead after all, they are not present except in bone form, in a glass case, for people to stare at. Like the Thylacine bones, the ones that were stared at for years, the ones they raided for the DNA to make the Thylacine clone.

Crowds visited. A documentary was made. Prizes were awarded. Then what happened? The Thylacine disappeared. It vanished. One day it was there, in solitude, in singleness, in its cage, or rather its large tastefully landscaped compound, running round and around as if looking for something, and then it was gone. It didn't die of solitude, however. It was sold. A bent scientist retired to Bermuda on the proceeds. A very rich person with refined tastes ate the Thylacine. He ate it in the form of a ragout. He had a yen for the unique, he wanted to be the only person ever to eat a Thylacine. It did not taste very good, despite the care taken in the preparation of it — well, there were no recipes — but it tasted very expensive, and the man who ate it wrote in his secret diary that it was good enough value for the money.

The Animals Reject Their Names and Things Return to Their Origins

I.

It was the bear who began it. Said,
I'm getting out from under.
I am not Bear, l'Ours, Ursus, Bär
or any other syllables
you've pinned on me.
Forget the chateau tapestries
in which I'm led in embroidered chains.
and the scarlet glories of the hunt
that was only glorious for you,
you with your clubs and bludgeons.

———

Forget the fairy tales, in which I was
your shaggy puppet, prince in hairshirt, surrogate
for human demons.
I'm not your coat, rug, glass-eyed trophy head,
plush bedtime toy, and that's not me
in outer space with my spangled cub.
I'm not your totem; I refuse
to dance in your circuses; you cannot carve
my soul in stone.

I renounce metaphor: I am not
child-stealer, shape-changer,
old garbage-eater, and you can stuff
simile also: unpeeled,
I am not *like a man*.

I take back what you have stolen,
and in your languages I announce
I am now nameless.
My true name is a growl.

———

(Come to think of it, I am not
a British headdress either:
I do not signify bravery.
I want to go back to eating salmon
without all this military responsibility.)

I follow suit, said the lion,
vacating his coats of arms
and movie logos; and the eagle said,
Get me off this flag.

II.

At this the dictionaries began to untwist,
and time stalled and reversed;
the sweaters wound back into their balls of wool,
which rolled bleating out into the meadows;
the perfumes returned to France
and old men there fell sweetly dead
from a surfeit of aroma.
Priests gave their dresses up again
to the women, and the women
ditched their alligator shoes in a hurry
before their former owners turned up to claim them.

———

The violins of the East Coast shores
took flight from the fingers of their players,
sucking in waltzes, laments, and reels,
landed in Scotland, fell apart
with wailing into their own wood and sinew
and vanished into the trees
and into the guts and howls of long-dead cats
and the tails of knackered horses.
Songs crammed themselves back down
the throats of their singers,
and a billion computers blew apart
and homed in chip by chip
on the brains of the inventors.

Squashed mice were shot backwards out of traps,
brides and grooms uncoupled like shunting
    trains,
tins of sardines exploded, releasing their
    wiggling shoals;
dinosaur bones whizzed like missiles
out of museums back to the badlands,
and bullets flew sizzling into their guns.
Glass beads popped off gowns and moccasins

and fell on Italy in a hail of dangerous colour,
as white people disappeared over the Atlantic
in a whoosh of pollution, vainly clutching
their power tools, car keys, and lawn mowers
which dove like metal fish back into the mines;
black people too, recapturing syncopation;
all flowers were suctioned budwise into their
    stems.
The Native peoples made speedy clearance work
of cowboys and longhorns, but then took off
westward instead, chanting goodbye
to ancestral plains, which were reclaimed
by shaggy mastodons and the precursors of
    horses
and everywhere
the children shrank and began to
drop teeth and grow hair.

III.

Well, there were suddenly a lot more flamingos
before they in their turn became eggs,
while people's bodies reverted through their own
flesh genealogies like stepping stones,

man woman man, container into contained,
shedding language and gathering themselves in,
skein after skein of protoplasm

until there was only one of them,
alone at the first naming;
but the streetwise animals, forewarned
and having learned the diverse meanings
of the word *dominion*,
did not show up,
and Adam, inarticulate, deprived
of his arsenal of proper nouns,
returned to mud

and mud itself became lava
and lava the uncooled earth
and the uncooled earth a swirl of white-hot
energy, and the energy jammed itself
into its own potential, and swirled
like fluorescent bathwater
down a non-existent wormhole.

IV.

I could end this with a moral,
as if this were a fable about animals,
though no fables are really about animals.

I could say: Don't offend the bear,
don't tell bad jokes about him,
have compassion on his bear heart;
I could say, Think twice
before you speak.
I could say, Don't take the name
of anything in vain.

But it's far too late for that,
because you can't read this,
because you can't remember the word for *read*,
because you are dizzy with aphasia,

because the page darkens and ripples
because it is liquid and unbroken,

because God has bitten his own tongue
and the first bright word of creation
hovers in the formless void
unspoken

Three Novels I Won't Write Soon

1. WORM ZERO

In this novel all the worms die. That would include the nematodes. Also anything wormlike in shape, though it may not be a worm proper. Should grubs be included? Should maggots? I'll know better once I get thoroughly into this thing.

Worms, anyway. Those in the earth, and those in the water. Those inside fish. Those inside dogs. Those inside people, such as pinworms, roundworms, and tapeworms. They die, each and every one. It's not all downside.

Or it's not all downside at first. But quite soon — because the earthworms are now defunct, and that's important — the soil is no longer circulating in the usual fashion. Worm dung is no longer extruded at the surface, worm-holes no longer allow rain to penetrate. Valuable nutrients remain sealed in layers of subsoil. Formerly productive fields turn to granite. Crops become stunted and then won't grow at all. Famine gets going.

Who shall we follow in the course of this doleful story? I vote for Chris and Amanda. They are a nice young couple who've had great sex in Chapter One, or possibly Chapter Two. Then realization has dawned on them, ruining their plans to renovate their kitchen and install a new round eco-friendly refrigerator that pops up out of the kitchen counter.

They flee to their summer cottage, as civic order breaks down in the once-thriving town where they live and people start eating their cats and goldfish and the dried ornamental sunflowers in their dining-room floral arrangements.

Amanda, who is the optimist of the pair, tries to grow some Tiny Tim tomatoes in the pathetic little patch of ground they once used only for petunias. Chris is a realist. He looks disaster squarely in its wormless face. (Yes — it's come to me! — the maggots have perished as well, which explains the various animal carcasses littering the cottage premises, gnawed on by crows and such, but not cleaned up neatly the way the maggots would once have done it.)

Last scene: Amanda is trying to poke holes in the flint-hard soil with a knitting needle. Chris comes out of the house. He has a cup containing their last scrapings of decaf instant coffee. "At least we're together," says Amanda.

Or should I have Chris yell, "Where are you, fucking worms, when we need you most?"

————

Maybe Amanda should yell it. That would be unexpected, and might show that her character has developed.

Now that this has happened – this cathartic, revealing, and somehow inspiriting yell – a small, still-wriggling worm might be discovered in the corner of the garden, copulating with itself. It would sound a note of plangent hope. I always like to end on those.

2. SPONGEDEATH

In this novel, a sponge located on a reef near the coast of Florida begins to grow at a very rapid rate. Soon it has reached the shore and is oozing inland, swallowing beach condos and gated communities as it goes. Nothing is able to stop it. It shows no respect for road-blocks, state police, or even bombs. A sponge on the rampage is a formidable foe. It has no central nervous system, not like us.

————

"It's not like us," says Chris, from the top of his condo, where he has gone with his binoculars to reconnoitre. Amanda clings to him fearfully. What a shame this is — they just bought the condo, in which they had great sex in Chapter One, and now look. All that decor gone to waste.

"Could we sprinkle salt on it?" Amanda asks, with appealing hesitation.

"Honey, it's not a slug," says Chris masterfully.

Should these be his last words? Should the sponge fall upon him with a soft but deadly glop? Or should he be allowed to defeat the monstrous bath accessory and save the day, for Florida, for America, and ultimately for humanity? The latter would be my own inclination.

But until I know the answer to this question — until I'm convinced, in my heart, that the human spirit has the wherewithal to go head to headless against this malevolent wad of cellulose – because as a writer loyal to the truth of the inner self you can't fake these things – it might be as well not to begin.

3. BEETLEPLUNGE

I heard it as if in a dream. "Beetleplunge." I often get such insights, such gifts from the Unknown, They just come to me. As this one came.

That word – if it is a word – might look quite stunning on the jacket of a book. Should it be "Beetle Plunge," two words? Or possibly "Beetle Plummet?" Or perhaps "Beetle Descent," which might sound more literary?

Let's think outside the box. Scrap the title! This is now a novel without a name. Immediately I am freed from the necessity of having to do something about the beetles. I saw them so clearly when I was first thinking about this book – all the beetles in the world plunging over a cliff, like lemmings, driven by some mysterious instinct gone wrong – but they did pose a problem: that is, what was to follow as a result?

Maybe I misheard. Maybe it was "Bottle Plunge." Maybe it was Chris and Amanda, in Chris's green Volkswagen, being forced off the road, and perilously close to the edge of an escarpment, by a black Mercedes driven by Amanda's drunken husband. Chris and Amanda had great sex in Chapter One, but Amanda's husband arrived in Chapter Two, in the Mercedes, just as Chris – who is their student gardener, at the gated community – was giving Amanda a post-coital explanation of the infestation of Coleoptera (red and black, with orange mandibles) currently ravaging the herbaceous borders.

As Chris was pronouncing the word *ravaging*, the husband sprang in through the French doors, in an advanced state of inebriation, with murder in his heart. Chris grabbed Amanda by the hand and made a dash for his own battered vehicle, a green Ford pickup: I've reconfigured the Volkswagen, it wasn't muscular enough. Cut to the chase. (Chris will drive very skilfully despite the distracting screams let out by Amanda, and he will swerve at the last moment, and the husband, whom we have never liked – he was a dishonest oil-and-gas executive and a sadistic foot fetishist – will go over the cliff instead. Chris and Amanda will end up shakily but gratefully in each other's arms, exactly where we want them to be.)

But maybe it wasn't "Bottle Plunge." Now that I think of it, the phrase may have been "Brutal Purge."

Where does that get us? Down to earth. But which brutal purge? There are so many to choose from. Those in the past, those in the present, and, unfortunately, those yet to come. Anyway, if it's "Brutal Purge," I can't see a way forward. Chris and Amanda are very likeable. They have straight teeth, trim waists, clean socks, and the best of intentions. They don't belong in a book like that, and if they stray into it by accident they won't come out of it alive.

Take Charge

I)

– Sir, their cannons have blown a hole in the ship. It's below the waterline. Water is pouring into the hold, Sir.

– Don't just stand there, you blockhead! Cut a piece of canvas, dive down, patch it!

– Sir, I can't swim.

– Bloody hell and damn your eyes, what wetnurse let you go to sea? No help for it, I'll have to do it myself. Hold my jacket. Put out that fire. Clear away those spars.

– Sir, my leg's been shot off.

– Well do the best you can.

II)

— Sir, their anti-tank missiles have shredded the left tread on our tank.

— Don't just sit there, you nitwit! Take a wrench, crawl underneath the tank, fix it!

— Sir, I'm a gunner, not a mechanic. Anyway that wouldn't work.

— Why in hell do they send me useless twits like you? No help for it, I'll have to do it myself. Cover me with your machine gun. Stand by with grenades. Hand me that spanner.

— Sir, my arm's been burnt off.

— Well do the best you can.

III)

— Sir, their diabolical worm virus has infected our missile command system. It's eating the software like candy.

— Don't just lounge there, you dickhead! Get going with the firewalls, or whatever you use.

— Sir, I'm a screen monitor, not a troubleshooter.

— Shit in a bucket, what do they think we're running here, a beauty parlour? If you can't do it, where's the nerdy spot-faced geek who can?

— Sir, it was him wrote the virus. He was not a team player, Sir. The missiles have already launched and they're heading straight for us.

— No help for it, I'll have to do it myself. Hand me that sledgehammer.

— Sir, we've got sixty seconds.

— Well do the best you can.

IV)

— Sir, the makorin has malfunctioned and set off the pizzlewhistle. That has saddammed the glopzoid plapoo-dle. It may be the work of hostile nanobacons.

— Don't just hover there, you clonedrone! Dopple the magmatron, reboot the fragebender, and insert the hi-speed crockblade with the pessimal-point attachment! That'll captcha the nasty little biobots!

— Sir, the magmatron is not within my area of expertise.

— What pixelwit deployed you? No help for it, I'll have to do it myself. Hand me the mutesuck blandplaster!

— Sir, I have been brain-napped. My brain is in a jar in Uzbekistan, guarded by a phalanx of virtual gonk-warriors. I am speaking to you via simulation hologram.

— Well do the best you can.

V)

— Sir, the wild dogs have dug their way into the food cache and they're eating the winter supplies.

— Don't just squat there, you layabout! Pick up your stone axe and bash them on the head!

— Sir, these are not ordinary wild dogs. They are red-eyed demon-spirit dogs, sent by the angry ancestors. Anyway, my stone axe has a curse on it.

— By my mother's bones, what did I do to deserve such a useless duck-turd brother's nephew's son as you? No help for it, I'll have to do it myself. Recite the red-eyed demon-spirit dog-killing charm and hand me my consecrated sacred-fire-hardened spear.

— Sir, they've torn my throat out.

— Well do the best you can.

Post-Colonial

We all have them: the building with the dome, late
Victorian, solid masonry, stone lions in front of it; the
brick houses, three storey, with or without fretwork,
wood, or painted iron, which now bear the word *Historic*
on tasteful enamelled or bronze plaques and can be
visited most days except Monday; the roses, big ones, of
a variety that were not here before. Before what? Before
the ships landed, we all had ships landing; before the
men in beaver hats, sailor hats, top hats, hats anyway,
got out of the ships; before the Native inhabitants shot
the men in hats with arrows or befriended them and
saved them from starvation, we all had Native inhabitants. Arrows or not, it didn't stop the men in hats, or

not for long, and they had flags too, we all had flags, flags that were not the same flags as the flags we have now. The Native inhabitants did not have hats or flags, or not as such, and so something had to be done. There are the pictures of the things being done, the before and after pictures you might say, painted by the painters who turned up right on cue, we all had painters. They painted the Native inhabitants in their colourful, hatless attire, they painted the men in hats, they painted the wives and children of the man in hats, once they had wives and children, once they had three-storey brick houses to put them in. They painted the brave new animals and birds, plentiful then, they painted the landscapes, before and after, and sometimes during, with axes and fire busily at work, you can see some of these paintings in the Historic houses and some of them in the museums.

We go into the museums, where we muse. We muse about the time before, we muse about the something that was done, we muse about the Native inhabitants, who had a bad time of it at our hands despite arrows, or, conversely, despite helpfulness. They were ravaged by disease: nobody painted that. Also hunted down, shot, clubbed over the head, robbed, and so forth. We muse about these things and we feel terrible. *We did that*, we think, *to them*. We say the word *them*, believing we know what we mean by it; we say the word *we*, even though we were not born at the time, even though our parents were not born, even though the ancestors of our ancestors may have come from somewhere else entirely, some place with dubious hats and with a flag quite different from the one that was wafted ashore here, on the wind, on the ill wind that (we also muse) has blown us quite a lot of good. We eat well, the lights go on most of the time, the roof on the whole does not leak, the wheels turn round.

As for *them*, our capital cities have names made from their names, and so do our brands of beer, and some but not all of the items we fob off on tourists. We make free with the word *authentic*. We are enamoured of hyphens, as well: our word, their word, joined at the hip. Sometimes they turn up in our museums, without hats, in their colourful clothing from before, singing authentic songs, pretending to be themselves. It's a paying job. But at moments, from time to time, at dusk perhaps, when the moths and the night-blooming flowers come out, our hands smell of blood. Just the odd whiff. *We did that, to them.*

But who are *we* now, apart from the question *Who are we now?* We all share that question. Who are we, now, inside the *we* corral, the *we* palisade, the *we* fortress, and who are they? Is that *them*, landing in their illicit boats, at night? Is that them, sneaking in here with out-landish hats, with flags we can't even imagine? Should we befriend them or shoot them with arrows? What are their plans, immediate, long-term, and will these plans of theirs serve us right? It's a constant worry, this *we*, this *them*.

And there you have it, in one word, or possibly two: post-colonial.

Heritage House

The Heritage House is where we keep the Heritage. It wasn't built for that – it was once a place where people really lived – but the way things needed to be done in it was cumbersome, what with the water coming out of a well, and the light coming out of oil lamps and tallow candles, and the heat coming out of a stone fireplace, and then there were the chamber pots to be emptied and the tin bathtubs to be filled. Also it was so hard to keep the rooms clean. So people built newer houses, with plumbing and so forth, but the Heritage House was not torn down, and when we decided to have some Heritage we agreed that the Heritage House was a good place to store the stuff.

We spruced it up, of course: fresh paint, brass polish, floor wax. Women were hired to show people around: they are adept at smiling and giving explanations, and nodding. Among us, it is thought that if men perform too many of these activities their faces will crack all over and peel off, and there will be nothing but gristle underneath.

The people who visited the Heritage House were mostly women as well. They wanted the explanations that could be found there — why some chairs were higher than other chairs, in the days of Heritage, and who did the scrubbing of the tin bathtubs and the emptying of the chamber pots, and how the water used to make its way out of the well. They wanted to know how things got the way they are now, and they hoped that the explanations given by the smiling women in the Heritage House might help.

Men didn't care so much about those subjects, and so they didn't go. Also they said that Heritage ought to mean things that have been inherited, passed down from father to son as it were, but since nobody did the so-called heritage things any more, or even thought about them except when they were in the Heritage House getting nodded and smiled at and bored to death with explanations, Heritage House was a misnomer in the first place and they didn't see why they should have to pay taxes to keep the joint going.

Over time, the Heritage House filled up. It was such a convenient place to stash things you no longer had a use for but didn't want to throw out. More and more Heritage was crammed in. An annex was built, in the style of the original edifice, with a tea room in it where you could rest your feet and relax – Heritage could be exhausting – and more female guides were hired, and research was done on authentic costumes for them to wear. But then there was a change of government and funds were cut. Perhaps some of the Heritage should be disposed of, it was said. But by now there was so much Heritage jammed in there that just sorting it out would take much more money than anyone wanted to spend. So nothing was done.

I went to the Heritage House myself, the other week. It was in disrepair. The windows were opaque with dust, the front steps were a disgrace: it was clear to see that nothing had been scrubbed off or fixed up in years. I rang the rusted bell for a long time before anyone answered it. Finally the door opened. I could see a long hallway, piled to the ceiling with boxes and crates. Each box was labelled: CORSETS. MIXMASTERS. THUMB-SCREWS. CALCULATORS. LEATHER MASKS. CARPET SWEEPERS. CHASTITY BELTS. SHOE BRUSHES. MANA-CLES. ORANGE STICKS. MISCELLANEOUS.

From behind the door an old woman appeared. She was wearing a chenille bathrobe. She let me in, pushing aside a stack of yellowing newspapers. The place stank of mouse droppings and mildew.

She nodded at me, she smiled. She hadn't lost the knack. Then she launched into a stream of explanations; but the language she spoke was obsolete, and I couldn't make out a word.

Bring Back Mom: An Invocation

Bring back Mom,
bread-baking Mom, in her crisp gingham apron
just like the aprons we sewed for her
in our Home Economics classes
and gave to her for a surprise
on Mother's Day —

Mom, who didn't have a job
because why would she need one,
who made our school lunches —
the tuna sandwich, the apple,

the oatmeal cookies wrapped in wax paper –
with the rubber band she'd saved in a jar;
who was always home when we got there
doing the ironing
or something equally boring,

who smiled the weak smile of a trapped drudge
as we slid in past her,
heading for the phone,
filled with surliness and contempt
and the resolve never to be like her.

Bring back Mom.
who wanted to be a concert pianist
but never had the chance
and made us take piano lessons,
which we resented –

Mom, whose aspic rings
and Jello salads we ate with greed,
though later derided –
pot-roasting Mom, expert with onions

though anxious in the face of garlic,
who received a brand-new frying pan
from us each Christmas –
just what she wanted –

Mom, her dark lipsticked mouth
smiling in the black-and-white
soap ads, the Aspirin ads, the toilet paper ads,
Mom, with her secret life
of headaches and stained washing
and irritated membranes –
Mom, who knew the dirt,
and hid the dirt, and did the dirty work,
and never saw herself
or us as clean enough –

and who believed
that there was other dirt
you shouldn't tell to children,
and didn't tell it,
which was dangerous only later.

———

We miss you, Mom,
though you were reviled to great profit
in magazines and books
for ruining your children
— that would be us —
by not loving them enough,
by loving them too much,
by wanting too much love from them,
by some failure of love —

(Mom, whose husband left her
for his secretary and paid alimony,
Mom, who drank in solitude
in the afternoons, watching TV,
who dyed her hair an implausible
shade of red, who flirted
with her friends' husbands at parties,
trying with all her might
not to sink below the line
between chin up and despair —

and who was carted away
and locked up, because one day

she began screaming and wouldn't stop,
and did something very bad
with the kitchen scissors –

But that wasn't you, not you, not
the Mom we had in mind, it was
the nutty lady down the street –
it was just some lady
who became a casualty
of unseen accidents,
and then a lurid story . . .)

Come back, come back, oh Mom,
from craziness or death
or our own damaged memory –
appear as you were:

Queen of the waffle iron,
generous dispenser of toothpaste,
sorceress of Mercurochrome,
player of games of smoky bridge
at which you won second-prize dishtowels,

brooder over the darning egg
that hatched nothing but socks,
boiler of horrible porridge –
climb back onto the cake-mix package,
look brisk and competent, the way you used to –

If only we could call you –
Here Mom, Here Mom –
and you would come clip-clopping
on your daytime Cuban heels,
smelling of sink and lilac,
(your bum encased in the foundation garment
you'd peel off at night
with a sigh like a marsh exhaling),
saying, *What is it now*,
and we could catch you
in a net, and cage you
in your bungalow, where you belong,
and make you stay –

Then everything would be all right
the way it was when we could play
till after dark on spring evenings,

then sleep without fear
because you threw yourself in front of the fear
and stopped it with your body —

And there you'll be, in your cotton housecoat,
holding a wooden peg
between your teeth, as the washing flaps
on the clothesline you once briefly considered
hanging yourself with —

but forget that! There you'll be,
singing a song of your own youth
as though no time has passed,
and we can be careless again,
and embarrassed by you,
and ignore you as we used to,

and the holes in the world will be mended.

III.

Horatio's Version

Absent thee from felicity awhile, and in this harsh world
draw thy breath in pain to tell my story . . .

These were Hamlet's last words to me. Well, almost the last. I didn't know at the time that this wasn't a request but a command – in effect, a clever and twisted curse. I would be doomed to stay alive until I *did* tell the story. Which is why you are reading my own words, in this very newspaper, today.

Yes, this is Horatio speaking: friend, confidant, ear-for-loan, eternal bystander at the festivities and debacles of the great and bloodthirsty. I have to say that I did my best as second banana during the Elsinore affair. I listened to Hamlet's outpourings, which at times bordered on lunacy; I sympathized; I offered what I hoped was sage advice. And then I got stuck with cleaning up the not inconsiderable mess.

Or not so much cleaning it up: wrapping it up. I was supposed to set down the events truthfully, as they had occurred, though showing Hamlet in a more or less favourable light, the light that shines on every protagonist. I hoped to wring some poetry out of these events, darkish poetry it would have to be. Perhaps I could add some philosophical musings about the human condition. I also hoped to come up with a plausible resolution to the story.

But what *was* the story? It was a tale of revenge, that much was clear. A wrong had been done, or it appeared to have been done. Hamlet said, as I recall, "O cursed spite that ever I was born to set it right," or something like that. But through morose dithering combined with sudden rash actions, he ended up killing quite a few more people than ought to have been killed, even according to the rather loose guidelines of honour as then constituted.

This often happens, as I've observed during the course of my now entirely too-long life. The Hatfields and the McCoys go at it, turn and turn about, until no one's left standing. Countries are similar. "Two wrongs don't make a right," I have often said while standing deliberately in the line of fire during these small, medium, and large payback events, but few have ever listened to me. An eye for an eye is their idea. A head for a head, a bomb for a bomb, a city for a city. Human beings — I've observed — are hot-wired for scorekeeping, and since they like to win, they're always going one better than the other fellow.

Excuse me. Not one better. One more.

I started out well enough at the outset. I found a fresh piece of parchment, I ground some ink. *Once upon a time there was a well-meaning but knotted-up prince called Hamlet*, I wrote. But that didn't sound quite right. Then I thought I might do it as a sort of play. *Elsinore. A Platform before the Castle*, I wrote. Then I dried up.

Trouble is, I started thinking about the story behind the story, which was not that Claudius had murdered Hamlet the Elder, but that Hamlet the Elder had murdered another king called Fortinbras. Well, not murdered exactly: slain in single combat, thus getting hold of a wad of Fortinbras territory. But the upshot of all of Hamlet Junior's machinations was that he himself ended up dead and Fortinbras the Second got hold of everything – not only his father's lost lands, but all of Hamlet's lands as well.

So if it was a revenge story it was a strange revenge. The only person to benefit from it was someone who hadn't been directly involved. That often happens too, I've noticed. Maybe instead of being a revenger's tragedy the Hamlet saga was a story about subconscious guilt – Hamlet realizes the Hamlet family has done dirt to the Fortinbras clan, and obliterates his own kinfolk and scuppers his inheritance in a spectacular act of self-sabotage.

While I was chewing on my quill, dozens of years went by. Then some jumped-up English playwright chose to dramatize this whole fracas. I was annoyed – he hadn't even been alive at the time, and he put in a bunch of stuff he couldn't possibly have known anything about. If he'd come to me I might have set him straight; but he didn't, and he published first. He filched my material and appropriated my voice and exploited a human tragedy that was really none of his business.

Anyway his play was too long.

My own writer's block got worse than ever. Hamlet's well-known procrastination had rubbed off on me. I began asking difficult questions. *Why me? Why should I have to write* Hamlet's *story? Why not my own?* But there's nothing much to mine, really. Come to think of it, is there anything much to Hamlet's? By this time we were well into the seventeenth century, and Oliver Cromwell had gone on the rampage, and Charles the First had had his head cut off, and thousands of soldiers and civilians had died cruel and ghastly deaths, with their intestines wound out of their bodies and their heads stuck up on stakes. I'd seen a lot of that up close, so a few slashed and drowned and poisoned bodies littering the Danish court were no longer very horrifying to me by comparison.

Somehow I no longer wanted to tell Hamlet's story. I wanted to tell something a little more – what's the term? Human, inhuman? Something bigger. But statistics pall after a time. We're not programmed to register more than a hundred corpses. In heaps they simply become a landscape feature.

So I went back to the stories of individuals. I've covered the ground, I can tell you. The French Revolution, the Terror, the slave trade, the Spanish wars, Australia, Cuba, North America, Africa, Mexico, Russia, Vietnam, the Middle East, Cambodia – you name it, I was there. Sometimes I was a peddler of supplies, sometimes a dispatch runner, sometimes a neutral observer, sometimes a provider of aid; more recently I've been working for the newspapers. I've talked to famine victims, war orphans, survivors of massacres and rapes, perpetrators of them – all sorts of people, with clean hands and dirty.

You've heard of injustice collecting? That's what I've become – an injustice collector. It's like a tax collector, only there's nothing to be done with the injustices once you've collected them except to pass them on, as best you can; though there's always the possibility that merely telling such stories will make people angry and thus give rise to other injustices. Still, after four centuries, I think I'm prepared to speak. To tell how things are, now, on this earth. Finally, I'm ready to begin.

So shall you hear of carnal, bloody, and unnatural acts; of accidental judgments, casual slaughters; of deaths put on by cunning and forced cause; and, in the upshot, purposes mistook, fall'n on the inventors' heads.

All this can I truly deliver.

King Log in Exile

After he had been deposed by the frogs, King Log lay disconsolately among the ferns and dead leaves a short distance from the pond. He'd had only enough energy to roll that far: he'd been King of the Pond for so long that he was heavily waterlogged. In the distance he could hear the jubilant croaking and the joyful trilling that signalled the coronation of his celebrated replacement, the experienced and efficient King Stork; and then – it seemed but a mini-second later – the shrieks of terror and the splashes of panic as King Stork set about spearing and gobbling up his new subjects.

King Log – ex–King Log – sighed. It was a squelchy sigh, the sigh of a damp hunk of wood that has been stepped on. What had he done wrong? Nothing. He himself had not murdered his citizens, as the Stork King was now doing. It was true he had done nothing right, either. He had done – in a word – nothing.

But surely his had been a benevolent inertia. As he'd drifted here and there, borne by the sluggish currents of the pond, tadpoles had sheltered beneath him and nibbled the algae that grew on him, and adult frogs had sunbathed on his back. Why then had he been so ignominiously dumped? In a *coup d'état* orchestrated by foreign powers, it went without saying; though certain factions among the frogs – stirred up by outside agitators – had been denouncing him for some time. They'd said a strong leader was needed. Well, now they had one.

There'd been that minor trade deal, of course. He'd signed it under duress, though nobody'd held a gun to his head, or what passed for his head. And hadn't it benefited the pond? There had been a sharp upturn in exports, the chief commodity being frogs' legs. But he himself had never been directly involved. He'd just been a facilitator. He'd tucked his cut of the profits away in a Swiss bank account, just in case.

Now the frogs were blaming him for the depredations of the Stork King. If King Log had been a better king himself, they were yelling – if he hadn't let the rot set in – none of this would have happened.

He knew he couldn't stay in the vicinity of the pond much longer. He must not give in to *anomie*. Already there were puffballs growing out of him, and under his bark the grubs were at work. He trundled away through the woods, the cries of amphibian anguish receding behind him. Served them right, he thought, sadly and a little bitterly.

King Log has retired to a villa in the Alps, where he is at present sprouting a fine crop of shitake mushrooms and working on his memoirs, one word at a time. Logs write slowly, and log kings more slowly than most. He has engaged a meditation guru who encourages him to visualize himself as a large pencil, but he can only get as far as the eraser.

He misses the old days. He misses the lapping of the water in the breeze, the rustling of the bulrushes. He misses the choruses of praise sung to him by the frogs in the pink light of evening. Nobody sings to him now.

Meanwhile the Stork King has eaten all the frogs and sold the tadpoles into sexual slavery. Now he is draining the pond. Soon it will be turned into desirable residential estates.

Faster

Walking was not fast enough, so we ran. Running was not fast enough, so we galloped. Galloping was not fast enough, so we sailed. Sailing was not fast enough, so we rolled merrily along on long metal tracks. Long metal tracks were not fast enough, so we drove. Driving was not fast enough, so we flew.

Flying isn't fast enough, not fast enough for us. We want to get there faster. Get where? Wherever we are not. But a human soul can only go as fast as a man can walk, they used to say. In that case, where are all the souls? Left behind. They wander here and there, slowly, dim lights flickering in the marshes at night, looking for us. But they're not nearly fast enough, not for us, we're way ahead of them, they'll never catch up. That's why we can go so fast: our souls don't weigh us down.

Eating the Birds

We ate the birds. We ate them. We wanted their songs to flow up through our throats and burst out of our mouths, and so we ate them. We wanted their feathers to bud from our flesh. We wanted their wings, we wanted to fly as they did, soar freely among the treetops and the clouds, and so we ate them. We speared them, we clubbed them, we tangled their feet in glue, we netted them, we spitted them, we threw them onto hot coals, and all for love, because we loved them. We wanted to be one with them. We wanted to hatch out of clean, smooth, beautiful eggs, as they did, back when we were young and agile and innocent of cause and effect, we did not want the mess of being born, and so we crammed the

birds into our gullets, feathers and all, but it was no use, we couldn't sing, not effortlessly as they do, we can't fly, not without smoke and metal, and as for the eggs we don't stand a chance. We're mired in gravity, we're earthbound. We're ankle-deep in blood, and all because we ate the birds, we ate them a long time ago, when we still had the power to say no.

Something Has Happened

Something has happened. But how? Was it overnight, or has it been creeping up on us and we've only just noticed? It's the girls, the young and pretty girls. They used to sing like sirens, like mermaids, all sweet and liquid, breezy melodies, wavy melodies, but now they're shorn of melody, though their mouths open and close as before. Have their tongues been cut out?

This is true as well of the cries of babies, the wailing at funerals, the screams that used to arise, especially at night, from the mad, from the tortured. It's the same thing with the birds: flying as before, spreading out their feathers as before, heads thrown back, beaks gaping, but they're mute. Mute, or muted? Who has been at work, with a great carpet of invisible snow that blots out sound?

Listen: the leaves no longer rustle, the wind no longer sighs, our hearts no longer beat. They've fallen silent. Fallen, as if into the earth. Or is it we who have fallen? Perhaps it's not the world that is soundless but we who are deaf. What membrane seals us off, from the music we used to dance to? Why can't we hear?

Nightingale

People die, and then they come back at night when you're asleep. By the time you're my age this happens more frequently. In the dream you know they're dead; funny thing is, they know it too. The usual places are a boat or a forest, less often a cabin or an isolated farmhouse, and, even more rarely, a room. If a room, there's often a window; if a window, there will be curtains — white — or heavy draperies, also white. Never venetian blinds: they don't like that kind of lighting, the day or night falling in slantwise through the slats. It makes them flicker even more than they normally do.

Sometimes they're friends, and they want you to know they're all right. That kind might make a remark

or two, nothing earth-shattering. It's like the screen when you turn off the television, one of them said — it's just a loss of contact. Another one — the setting was a woodland walk, in fall, orange and yellow leaves, that crisp smell — this one said, Isn't it beautiful?

Some don't say anything. They might smile, they might not; they might turn away once they know you've seen them. They want you to see them: that's the point. They want you to know they're still around and they can't be forgotten or dismissed.

Procne turned up the other night. Got in through the window, as she always does. Right away I wished I'd taken a sleeping pill: that would have shut her out. But you can't take pills all the time, and she waits. She waits until I'm unconscious.

You shouldn't have let him lock me up in that shack, she said.

The location was a room; the window in question had white curtains. We've been through this before, I said. You weren't locked up. You could have opened the door. Anyway, I didn't know.

You knew, she said. You repressed it, but you must have known.

I knew you'd been his first wife, I said. Everyone knew that. But according to him you were dead.

That's what they wanted you to think, she said. I might as well have been, but I wasn't. Meanwhile, you were getting ready to take my place.

I had to, I said. I had to get married. He raped me. What else could I have done? Don't tell me you were jealous.

Jealous? she said. She gave a kind of caw. Not for an instant! I knew his dirty ways, he could never leave me alone. Believe me, you were welcome to that part of it. I only wish he hadn't cut out my tongue.

That is a lie, I said. He never did that. You made the decision not to speak, is all. The tongue part of the story is a misreading of a temple wall painting, that's what people say now. Those things weren't tongues, they were laurel leaves for the priestess, so she could hallucinate, and prophesy, and –

You and your archeology, said Procne. He cut out my tongue, all right. He knew I'd tell stories.

Maybe he had his reasons, I said. If he did cut out your tongue. I'm sorry, I didn't mean that. I'm not excusing his behaviour. It wasn't good. None of us behaved very well, and I regret that now. The two of us never got along when we were young, but you were always my sister and I loved you. That's why he kept you a secret from me.

I knew you wouldn't excuse it. His behaviour, I mean. That's why I sent you the message – to let you know I wasn't dead after all. *Procne is among the slaves*, is all it said. I didn't write, *Set me free*, I didn't want to influence you one way or the other. I didn't want you taking any risks on my behalf.

Then why did you send me the message?

I wanted you to avoid the mistakes I made, that's all.

What mistakes?

In answer she lifted up her hands. They were wet, they glistened. Our son, she said. I couldn't stop myself.

The window was open at the bottom, there was a breeze, the curtains were blowing. The air smelled of apple blossom. I wish you'd leave me alone, I say. It's over, it's long ago. You're dead now, and he's dead, and there's nothing I can do. It's only a story now and I'm too old to listen to it.

You're never too old, says Procne. Her voice is so sad. Then she starts turning into a bird, the way she always does, and when I look down the same thing is happening to me. This is when I remember the two of us running,

running away from him, and I know in the dream that I'm dead too, because at the end of the story he killed us both.

Then Procne flies out through the window, and so do I. It's night, a forest, a moon. We land on a branch. It's at this moment, in the dream, that I begin to sing. A long liquid song, a high requiem, the story of the story of the story.

Or is the voice hers? Hard to tell.

A man standing underneath our tree says, *Grief.*

Warlords

To be a warlord – that's a boy's dream everywhere. Point a finger, say Bang, and thousands die. Most of these sharpshooters grow up to become dentists. But if you're born under the rule of a warlord, you have only three futures. To be a warrior and die in the service of the warlord. To depose the warlord and become the warlord yourself. To be one who by definition cannot be a warrior – a woman, a priest, a one-legged tailor. But you are shut up inside the warlord's territorial periphery, which at times feels like a protecting wall and at other times like a dungeon. In there, you can live what is thought of – in there – as a normal life, as long as you wave the warlord's flag, pay the warlord's taxes, bribe the warlord's henchmen, grovel at the feet of the warlord's relatives, and avoid all negative comments about the warlord himself, as he is known to be touchy.

The warlord sits at the centre of his own power, inert but potent. Sycophants spoon food and good news into him; vulture-handlers handle his pet vultures; ruby-counters count his rubies; beautiful damsels lick his toes. Concentric rings of warriors encircle him. The outermost ring is most at risk. The men there bristle with hardware; they look like many-bladed jackknives, the kind with the corkscrew, the nail file, and the awl, and it is they who take the first risks, and are ground under the giant clanking wheels of the invading warlords. The next ring is made of slippery defences, labyrinthine corridors, trenches filled with pointed stakes, ambushes involving falling boulders and red-hot coals, very deadly but after a while not enough. The warriors who work this ring obey one single command: *Hold the gate!*

Hand-picked worldwide warriors form the inner circle. They are mercenaries, because you can't trust volunteers. They are the bodyguards, They guard the body. They're supposed to guard it with their deaths, they aren't supposed to live to tell the tale, but some do. The tale is about how, despite their best efforts or anyway their second best, the warlord's forces were finally overcome. How his cave, his tree, his tower, his castle, his city, his weapons factories, his prisons, his billiard rooms went up in flames. How the invading army drank up all his champagne and took baths in his bathtubs. How his concubines were gang-raped on the rooftops, his wives dismembered, his children blinded, to the delighted howls of the crowd, who now claim never to have liked the warlord anyway. How he himself was roasted, skewered, blown up, beheaded, hanged upside down, forced into bankruptcy. How his statues were toppled and sold as scrap, or else as kitschy souvenirs.

What point in continuing, after that? With being a hand-picked worldwide warrior. No future in it. No prestige. Scramble out of the uniform, the trappings, the trap; run for your life, through the dank forest, across the prickly desert, up the icy mountains, leaving blood footprints. When you've reached neutral territory, when you've stashed the loot hoisted from the warlord's mansion – well, he didn't have much use for it any more, did he? – and when you finally have a spare moment to sit down at a café with a cool drink, you rethink your occupation.

But your occupation's gone. You can't get another. Once you've fought for a warlord, any warlord, even a warlord committee, you can't forget. You can't learn anything else. Nothing can replace the adrenalin, the hellish but enlivening nightmares. Nothing — let's face it — is nearly as much fun as being a warlord's warrior. *Fun* taken in the broadest sense of the word, you understand.

Look over there. See that ropy-muscled old guy raking the lawn? The other one sweeping the sidewalk, the third hauling the trash? Warlord survivors, all of them. They're branded with invisible tattoos. Behind their eyes the embers smoulder. They're waiting. They're ready for the call.

The Tent

You're in a tent. It's vast and cold outside, very vast, very cold. It's a howling wilderness. There are rocks in it, and ice and sand, and deep boggy pits you could sink into without a trace. There are ruins as well, many ruins; in and around the ruins there are broken musical instruments, old bathtubs, bones of extinct land mammals, shoes minus their feet, auto parts. There are thorny shrubs, gnarled trees, high winds. But you have a small candle in your tent. You can keep warm.

Many things are howling out there, in the howling wilderness. Many people are howling. Some howl in grief because those they love have died or been killed, others howl in triumph because they have caused the loved ones of their enemies to die or be killed. Some howl to summon help, some howl for revenge, others howl for blood. The noise is deafening.

It's also frightening. Some of the howling is coming close to you, in your tent, where you crouch in silence, hoping you won't be seen. You're frightened for yourself, but especially for those you love. You want to protect them. You want to gather them inside your tent, for protection.

The trouble is, your tent is made of paper. Paper won't keep anything out. You know you must write on the walls, on the paper walls, on the inside of your tent. You must write upside down and backwards, you must cover every available space on the paper with writing. Some of the writing has to describe the howling that's going on outside, night and day, among the sand dunes and the ice chunks and the ruins and bones and so forth; it must tell the truth about the howling, but this is difficult to do because you can't see through the paper walls and so you can't be exact about the truth, and you don't want to go out there, out into the wilderness, to see exactly for yourself. Some of the writing has to be about your loved ones and the need you feel to protect them, and this is difficult as well because not all of them can hear the howling in the same way you do, some of them think it sounds like a picnic out there in the wilderness, like a big band, like a hot beach party, they resent being cooped up in such a cramped space with you and your small candle and your fearfulness and your annoying obsession with calligraphy, an obsession that makes no sense to them, and they keep trying to scramble out under the walls of the tent.

This doesn't stop you from your writing. You write as if your life depended on it, your life and theirs. You inscribe in shorthand their natures, their features, their habits, their histories; you change the names, of course, because you don't want to create evidence, you don't want to attract the wrong sort of attention to these loved ones of yours, some of whom — you're now discovering — are not people at all, but cities and landscapes, towns and lakes and clothing you used to wear and neighbourhood cafés and long-lost dogs. You don't want to attract the howlers, but they're attracted anyway, as if by a scent: the walls of the paper tent are so thin that they can see the light of your candle, they can see your outline, and naturally they're curious because you might be prey, you might be something they can kill and then howl over in celebration and then eat, one way or another. You're too conspicuous, you've made yourself conspicuous, you've given yourself away. They're coming closer, gathering together; they're taking time off from their howling to peer, to sniff around.

Why do you think this writing of yours, this grapho-mania in a flimsy cave, this scribbling back and forth and up and down over the walls of what is beginning to seem like a prison, is capable of protecting anyone at all? Yourself included. It's an illusion, the belief that your doodling is a kind of armour, a kind of charm, because no one knows better than you do how fragile your tent really is. Already there's a clomping of leather-covered feet, there's a scratching, there's a scrabbling, there's a sound of rasping breath. Wind comes in, your candle tips over and flares up, and a loose tent-flap catches fire, and through the widening black-edged gap you can see the eyes of the howlers, red and shining in the light from your burning paper shelter, but you keep on writing anyway because what else can you do?

Time Folds

Time folds, he said, meaning that as time goes on and on it buckles, in the extreme heat, in the extreme cold, and what is long past becomes closer. You can demonstrate this by pleating a ribbon and sticking a pin through: Point Two, once yards away from Point One, now lies just beside it. Is time/space like an accordion, but without the music? Was he making a statement about hard physics?

Or was he saying: Time folds its wings, at long last. Time folds its tents and silently steals way. Time folds you in its folds, as if you were a lamb and the lack of time a wolf.

Time folds you in the blanket of itself, it folds you tenderly and wraps you round, for where would you be without it? Time folds you in its arms and gives you one last kiss, and then it flattens you out and folds you up and tucks you away until it's time for you to become someone else's past time, and then time folds again.

Tree Baby

You remember this. No, you dreamed it. Your dream was
of choking, and sinking down, and blankness. You woke
from your nightmare and it had already happened.
Everything was gone. Everything, and everyone —
fathers, mothers, brothers, sisters, the cousins, the
tables and chairs and toys and beds — all swept away.
Nothing is left of them. Nothing remains but the erased
beach and the silence.

There is wreckage. You didn't see that, in your dream. A
jumble of smashed years, a heap of broken stories. The
stories look like wood and chunks of cement and twisted

metal. And sand, a lot of sand. Why is it they say *the sands of time*? You didn't know that yesterday but now you do. You know too much to say. What can be said? Language turns to rubble in your throat.

But look – there's a baby, stranded in a treetop, just as in those other dreams, the ones in which you can lift yourself off the earth and fly, and escape the roaring and crashing just behind you. A baby, alive, caught in a green cradle; and it's been rescued, after all. But its name has been lost, along with its tiny past.

What new name will they give it, this child? The one who escaped from your nightmare and floated lightly to a tree, and who looks around itself now with a baby's ordinary amazement? Now time starts up once more, now there is something that can be said: this child must be given a word. A password, a talisman of air, to help it through the many hard gates and shadow doorways ahead. It must be named, again.

———

Will they call it Catastrophe, will they call it Flotsam, will they call it Sorrow? Will they call it No-family, will they call it Bereft, will they call it Child-of-a-Tree? Or will they call it Astonishment, or Nevertheless, or Small Mercy?

Or will they call it Beginning?

But It Could Still

Things look bad: I admit it. They look worse than they've looked for years, for centuries. They look the worst ever. Perils loom on all sides. But it could still turn out all right. The child fell from the eighth-floor balcony, but there was a sheepdog underneath that leapt up and caught it in mid-air. A bystander took a picture, it was in the paper. The boy went under for the third time, but the mother — although she was reading a novel — heard a gurgling sound and ran down to the dock, and reached into the water, and pulled the boy up by his hair, and there was no brain damage. When the explosion occurred the young man was underneath the sink, fixing the plumbing, and so he was not injured. The girl survived the avalanche by making swimming motions with her arms. The father of two-year-old triplets who had cancer in every one of his organs watched a lot of comedy films and did Buddhist meditation and went into full remission, where he remains to this day. The airbags actually worked. The cheque did not bounce. The prescription drug company was not lying. The shark nudged the sailor's naked, bleeding leg, then turned away. The rapist got distracted in mid-rape, and his knife and his penis both retracted into him like the soft and delicate horns of a snail, and he went out for a coffee instead. The copy of Darwin's *Origin of Species* the soldier carried next to his heart stopped the oncoming machine-gun bullet. When he said, *My darling, you are the only woman I will adore forever*, he really meant it. As for her, despite the scowling and the cold shoulder and the unanswered phone, it turned out she'd loved him all along.

At this dim season of the year we hunger for such tales. Winter's tales, they are. We want to huddle round them, as if around a small but cheerful fire. The sun sets at four, the temperature plummets, the wind howls, the snow cascades down. Though you nearly froze your fingers off, you did get the tulips planted, just in time. In four months they'll come up, you have faith in that, and they'll look like the picture in the catalogue. In the brown earth there were already hundreds of small green shoots. You didn't know what they were — some sort of little bulb — but they were intending to grow, despite everything. What would you call them if they were in a story? Would they be happy endings, or happy beginnings? But they aren't in a story, and neither are you. You tucked them back under the mulch and the dead leaves, however. It was the right thing to do on the darkest day of the year.

Acknowledgements

Material in this collection has been previously published as follows:

"Our Cat Enters Heaven" in *Brick*; "Warlords" and "Voice" in *The Walrus*; "Take Charge," "King Log in Exile," "Salome Was a Dancer," and "Post-Colonial" in *Daedalus*; "Life Stories" and "Resources of the Ikarians" in *Short Story*; and "Chicken Little Goes Too Far" and "The Tent" in *Harper's Magazine*.

In addition, "Bottle," "It's Not Easy Being Half-Divine," and an earlier version of "Nightingale" appeared in a limited-edition booklet published in aid of the Harbourfront Reading Series; these three and "Take

ACKNOWLEDGMENTS

Charge," "King Log in Exile," "Thylacine Ragout," "Post-Colonial," "Faster," and "Bottle II" were published in a limited-edition booklet called *Bottle*, in aid of the Hay-On-Wye Festival in Wales; "Tree Baby," "But It Could Still," and "Something Has Happened" appeared in *New Beginnings*, an anthology published in support of the Indian Ocean Tsunami Earthquake charities; "Bottle" appeared in a German-language literary advent calendar called *Das Geschenk*; and "Chicken Little Goes Too Far" was auctioned in a holograph-illustrated edition of one, in aid of the World Wildlife Fund.

A Note About the Type

The text of this book is set in Filosofia, a typeface designed in 1996 by Zuzana Licko, cofounder, with her husband, Rudy VanderLans, of the font house Emigre. Filosofia is Licko's interpretation of Bodoni, showing her preference for a geometric Bodoni while also incorporating the slightly bulging, round serif endings which reflect Bodoni's origins in letterpress technology. It is a modern, legible font ideally suited for smaller-size text applications.